D1165043

HOW IT WAS

THE CRUSADES

Michael Hodges

B. T. Batsford Ltd, London

CONTENTS

First published 1995

Typeset by Goodfellow & Egan Ltd, Cambridge

and printed in Hong Kong

Published by
B. T. Batsford Ltd
4 Fitzhardinge Street
London W1H 0AH

A CIP catalogue record for this book is available from the British Library.

ISBN 0 7134 7436 X

Cover illustration: *Supplies being loaded for the Crusades.*

Frontispiece: *Pope Urban II preaching the first crusade at the Council of Clermont.*

INTRODUCTION

At its height the Roman Empire stretched from modern Turkey in the east to Scotland in the north, but its very size made it difficult for one emperor to control. In 330 AD, Emperor Constantine I divided the empire into two parts. The Western Roman Empire was governed from Rome, and the Eastern Empire from a new city founded by Constantine called New Rome or Constantinople. Usually, each part had its own emperor.

Over the next seven centuries the two empires drifted apart. The Western Empire became increasingly concerned with holding the imperial frontiers against barbarian invaders. At first these tribes were beaten back, bought off or assimilated into the Western Empire. In time, though, the barbarian thrusts became more determined. Gradually, the Western Empire broke up and in 476 AD Odoacer, a barbarian general, crowned himself King of Italy. Amidst the ruin of the Western Roman Empire, the Roman Catholic Church kept its existence and prestige. At the head of the Roman Church was the Pope (meaning father, or chief).

Meanwhile, the Eastern Empire prospered. It became increasingly independent of Rome and was very much influenced by Greek culture and values. After 1054, the Eastern Orthodox Churches no longer accepted the authority of the Pope. Constantinople was unrivalled by any other city in Europe and the Mediterranean region.

After the fall of the Western Roman Empire, the Eastern Roman Empire, better known as Byzantium, struggled for her own survival against the Persians (sixth and seventh centuries), the Arabs and then the Seljuk Turks. By the late eleventh century the various Muslim powers occupied the Byzantine possessions of Palestine, North Africa and much of Asia Minor. Among their gains were the great centres of early Christianity – Antioch, Alexandria, Ephesus, Caesarea and most symbolic of all, Jerusalem, where Jesus had lived, taught, healed and died.

Despite these territorial losses, Byzantium remained the dogged and respected defender of Christendom (Christian states in Europe) in the East, a position which was widely acknowledged because of her achievements as well as her historic origins and continued authority. Whenever possible, Byzantine's protection extended to the welfare of numerous Christian communities which survived in the Muslim-controlled Holy Places, and to the pilgrims on their way to Palestine.

Usually, Muslims were tolerant of Christians and Jews, whom Muslims saw as sharing important beliefs. Islam's sacred book, the Koran, contains passages from the Bible, and Jesus is recognized as the last great prophet before Mohammed.

Jerusalem was as sacred to Muslims as to Christians. When Caliph Omar captured Jerusalem in 638 AD he rode at once to the site of the Temple of Solomon, where Muslims believe Omar's friend, the prophet Mohammed, had risen to Heaven. Yet despite Islamic control of the city, 'Every year many Byzantines come here [Jerusalem] for pilgrimage. Even the emperor comes secretly,' wrote Nasir-i-Khosrau in his *Journey Through Syria and Palestine*, written in about the 11th century. Under Islamic law Christians and Jews were protected, though they paid more taxes.

The combination of Islamic tolerance and Byzantine diplomacy (and occasionally force) allowed Christians to live in the East without fear of attack: a delicate balance to be shattered by a new movement from the West – the Crusades.

This book follows the Crusaders in their campaigns against the Islamic forces, from the ill-fated People's Crusade to the fall of Constantinople in 1453, revealing not only base and noble qualities in the two warring sides, but also their ability to live in harmony in the state of Outremer.

Introductory quiz

Do you know?

Where the Crusaders came from?

How Muslims in their robes fought against the Crusaders in their armour?

The origins of the St John Ambulance Service?

Why the Franks started using soap?

Where the word 'assassin' comes from?

HOW THE CRUSADES BEGAN

In 1071 the Byzantine Empire suffered two crushing blows at the hands of the Seljuks, Turkish nomads who, after converting to Sunni Islam, had conquered what is now Iran and Iraq. Firstly, the Empire was defeated heavily at the battle of Manzikert, at the far edge of the Eastern Empire beyond the River Euphrates. From that point onwards Byzantium lost more and more land each year to the invaders, until its capital, Constantinople, was menaced. Worse still, Anatolia (modern Turkey), which had been the most important recruiting ground for the Empire's army, was overrun.

In 1071 the Seljuks also occupied Jerusalem. Their policy towards pilgrims and non-Muslims was more repressive than their predecessors. Byzantium was unable to protect pilgrims from Muslim harassment as they travelled through the Holy Land to Jerusalem.

Now that Byzantium was incapable of defending Christendom against this new Muslim threat, Alexius I, Emperor of Byzantium, made his fateful appeal in 1095 to Pope Urban II. The Emperor asked the Pope to encourage mercenary (hired) soldiers to go to Constantinople and help the Empire hold back the Islamic advance. The last thing the Pope wanted was for the Muslims to break through the eastern frontiers of Christendom and swarm through central Europe, as they had into France from Spain nearly 400 years before, until repulsed at the battle of Tours in 732 AD.

Therefore, that same year, 1095, Pope Urban preached his famous Crusade to a large and enthusiastic crowd of mostly humble people, gathered outside the town of Clermont in France. Urban played down the Emperor's plea for bands of mere mercenaries. Instead, he used the emotional appeal of the suffering of Christians in the Holy Land and the abuse of the sacred places in Jerusalem by the Muslims to launch huge armies from western Europe. The Pope urged Christians to recover Jerusalem, to destroy the Islamic presence in Palestine, to rescue their fellow and isolated Christians from the oppression of Muslim rule and to re-open the pilgrim routes through Palestine. None of these aims could succeed without the need to settle in the Holy Land.

Urban's objectives appealed to a wide cross-section of people. All were attracted to the opportunity of serving God by recapturing

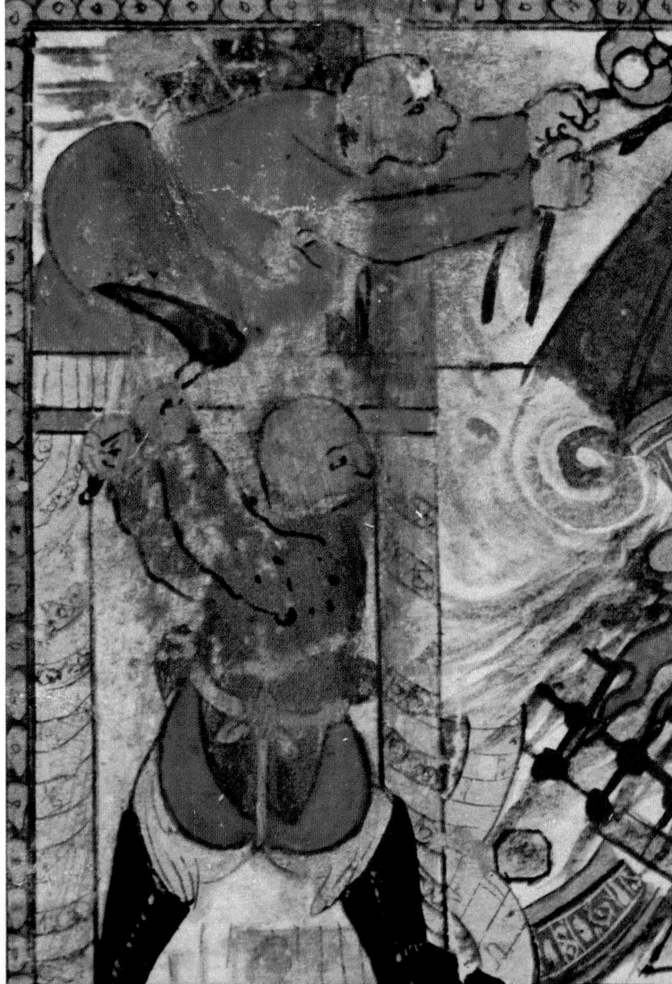

Jerusalem and by the Pope's assurances that Crusaders would go to Heaven if they died fighting the Muslim infidel (unbeliever). On top of that, Urban promised forgiveness of sins for those who joined the Crusade.

Europe was then enduring one of her most dismal times. Exceptional violence raged over the possession of land and castles between disaffected (discontented), landless and lawless younger sons of the nobility. Poorer people lived in terror of bad harvests, of famine and a new, strange disease, caused by mouldy rye, called 'holy fire' that could lead to madness. For some, the chance of starting a new life in Palestine was enough reason to escape from the hardship and a dead-end existence in Europe. Others intended to return to the West after the expedition achieved success. There also lurked the dread of disgrace and the fear of excommunication for any crusader who failed to keep his crusading vow of liberating Jerusalem and the Holy Land, and praying at the Church of the Holy Sepulchre.

Such was the enthusiasm that one chronicler, a monk called Fulcher of Chartres (page 7), marvelled when people tore their cloaks to bits, made crosses from them and pinned them on their chest and shoulders. The word crusade comes from the Latin word crux meaning a cross – in other words, the war of the cross.

Emperor Alexius was horrified once he realized that, instead of mercenaries whom he would pay and, therefore, control, organized armies were being assembled under their own leaders with the intention of capturing Jerusalem. The Crusade's objectives conflicted with generations of Byzantine imperial policy. Byzantium preferred to secure peace and prosperity in Palestine by exploiting divisions within the Muslim world, and to make treaties with one Muslim branch in order to check the aggression of another. A full-scále Crusade would unite the Muslim forces, threatening the Empire's stability and destroying years of careful diplomacy.

The Dome of the Rock, centre of Muslim pilgrimage in Jerusalem. It was the site of Muhammad's ascent to heaven.

The destruction of the Church of the Holy Sepulchre, built over Christ's tomb in Jerusalem, by Muslim forces in 1009.

HOW THE CRUSADES BEGAN

The People's Crusade

Before the First Crusade set out, a wandering priest called Peter the Hermit organized his own unofficial and ill-fated 'People's Crusade'. An inspired preacher but a hopeless leader, Peter virtually lost control of 'all the common people and knights, the chaste as well as the sinful; adulterers, homicides, perjurers, robbers', who plundered their way through central Europe to Constantinople. Abbot Guibert (1064–1125) described Peter as follows:

> **With his long face framed in a dirty old hood, he looked remarkably like the donkey he always rode . . . Whatever he did or said was regarded as little short of Divine, to such an extent that hairs were snatched from his mule as relics.**
>
> **(*Chronicle of the First Crusade*)**

Anna Comnena (see page 10) recorded the arrival of the People's Crusade in Constantinople:

> **Full of enthusiasm and ardour they thronged every highway, and with the warriors came a host of civilians carrying palms and bearing crosses on their shoulders. There were women and children, too . . .**
>
> **(*The Alexiad*, c.1140)**

An unknown Norman soldier who travelled with Peter, and later joined Bohemond, the Norman prince, wrote *The Deeds of the Franks* (*Gesta Francorum*). He observed Peter's Crusaders in Constantinople:

> **These Christians behaved abominably, sacking and burning the palaces of the City, and stealing lead from the roofs of churches and selling it to the Greeks [the Byzantines] so the Emperor was angry and ordered them to cross the Hellespont [the sea channel separating Constantinople (now Istanbul) from Asia Minor]**
>
> **(*The Deeds of the Franks*, c.1100)**

Muhammad ascending to heaven.

CAN YOU REMEMBER ?

Who Alexius was?
Where the Seljuks came from and what their religion was?
Why Alexius was horrified when he heard a Crusade was on its way to the Holy Land?

THINGS TO DO

1 Imagine you have heard Pope Urban's speech at Clermont. Write a letter to a relative who farms poor land, convincing him to join you on the Crusade.

2 The distance (on land) from Northern France to Palestine via Constantinople is approximately 3500 kilometres. If you walked an average of 25 kilometres a day how long would you take to get there? Imagine, however, you are a member of the People's Crusade. What problems might slow you down? (Think about roads, food and enemies.)

The People's Crusade was a disaster. While Peter negotiated with Alexius for supplies, in 1096 his Crusaders perished near Nicaea where the Seljuks had captured the only springs.

The crusaders bled their horses and asses and drank the blood. Others let down belts and clothes into a sewer and squeezed out the liquid into their mouths.

Anna Comnena wrote that the dead made a mountain of bones:

Some men of the same race as the slaughtered barbarians, later, when they were building a wall like those of a city, used the bones of the dead as pebbles to fill in the cracks. In a way the city became their tomb.

(*The Alexiad*, c.1140)

Abbot Guibert did not travel to the Holy Land himself – where do you think he got his information from?

Pope Urban's Appeal

Fulcher of Chartres, Chaplain to Count Baldwin (page 20), was the best educated and most reliable of the chroniclers, and he was present at Clermont. His chronicle was published in three instalments from 1101–27. In it he gives this version of Urban's appeal:

A grave report has come from the lands around Jerusalem and from the city of Constantinople . . . a foreign race, a race absolutely alien to God has invaded the land of those Christians, has reduced the people with sword, rapine and flame and has carried off some as captives to its own land, has cut down others by pitiable murder and has either completely razed churches of God to the ground or enslaved them to the practice of its own rites (religious customs) . . .

You oppressors of orphans, you robbers of widows, you homicides, you blasphemers, you plunderers of others' rights . . . go forward boldly as knights of Christ, hurrying swiftly to defend the Eastern [Christian] church . . . it is better for you to die in battle than to tolerate the abuse of your race and your holy places.

(*The Deeds of the Franks*, c.1100)

How does Pope Urban aim to divert fighting from Europe to Palestine?
What do you discover about the state of Europe?

CHECK YOUR UNDERSTANDING

Can you remember the meaning of the following?

mercenary
Christendom
excommunication
Pope
Crusade

Peter the Hermit, leader of the People's Crusade.

CRUSADERS AT CONSTANTINOPLE

While the People's Crusade met an unhappy end in Asia Minor, from all over Europe princes, knights and ordinary people streamed to Le Puy in central France. There, they took their Crusading vow before Adhemar, Bishop of Le Puy, who was the church leader of the Crusade. The leaders were influential princes who brought their own armies and travelled to Constantinople independently. From northern France came Godfrey of Lorraine accompanied by about 10,000 soldiers and his penniless younger brother, Baldwin. Baldwin took his family and probably intended not to return. At the time people thought Godfrey was the perfect Christian knight, though he was not above blackmailing Jews to raise money for his army. Although land prices had dropped, many Crusaders sold their estates or borrowed money in order to finance their costs.

The tough Bohemond and his nephew, Tancred, led the Norman army. This branch of the Normans had recently settled in south Italy after Bohemond's father, Robert Guiscard, had driven out the Byzantine inhabitants. Across the sea lay Byzantine territory, always tempting for the land-greedy Normans. Recent experience had taught Alexius that the Normans were cunning, dangerous and ambitious.

Raymond of Toulouse was the wealthiest of all the princes. By his marriage he was connected with the Spanish royalty. Raymond wanted to command the Crusade, but he lacked the ruthlessness of Bohemond and the inspiration of Godfrey. Raymond often quarrelled with the other princes, especially Bohemond.

The fourth army was under the collective leadership of Robert of Normandy, his cousin Robert of Flanders, and Stephen of Blois. Stephen was a peaceful man who had the misfortune to be married to the formidable Adela, daughter of William the Conqueror. It was a tense marriage, especially when Stephen returned in disgrace from the Holy Land.

Meanwhile, in Constantinople, Emperor Alexius heard reports of huge armies of Crusaders approaching his Empire with mounting dismay. Once the Crusaders crossed into Byzantium they began pillaging (robbing) the villages which stood in their way. Alexius sent his best imperial troops to escort the Crusaders and to provide food, at the same time keeping them under surveillance and providing an official welcome.

When the Crusaders reached Constantinople it didn't take long before they had sacked one suburb. And when Godfrey spoke of attacking Constantinople, Alexius was convinced that the Crusaders' aim was to take over his Empire. Alexius dared not allow the four armies to concentrate outside his capital. As each army arrived he transported it across the Bosphorus to the Asiatic shore.

Constantinople under siege by the Ottoman Turks in 1453. The city's capture in April of that year spelt the end of the Byzantine Empire.

(Left) *A Crusader wearing chain mail and a long surcoat as protection against the sun.*

Alexius did promise support and supplies for the re-conquest of Asia Minor. Advisers would travel with the Crusaders, guide the armies through the harsh and barren interior, and advise on tactics when fighting the Muslims. They would alert the Crusaders as to which Seljuk tribes were friendly and which were hostile. These distinctions meant nothing to the Crusaders, to whom all Muslims were the enemy.

Earlier Alexius made each leader promise that all land in Asia Minor lost after the battle of Manzikert (page 4) would be returned to Byzantium. Any land south of Asia Minor was left for the Crusaders to deal with as they thought best. The capture of Jerusalem was a pointless exercise to Alexius, and worse still, would destroy the relationship between Christians and Muslims. Recently, Alexius had signed a peace treaty with the Fatimid branch of Islam which controlled Egypt and, now, Jerusalem. He did not want to upset the Fatimids by associating himself too closely with the Crusaders whose aim to capture Jerusalem would clash with Fatimid interests.

CRUSADERS AT CONSTANTINOPLE

Anna Comnena

Anna Comnena was the eldest child of Alexius. Like her mother, Irene, she was an able, forceful and cultured woman who carried a lot of influence at the Byzantine court. She developed into a lively historian whose observations were sharp, though she always took the Byzantine point of view. Devoted to her father, she failed, however, to persuade Alexius on his death-bed to favour her husband as his heir. For this intrigue she spent years in a nunnery where, 40 years later, aged 54, she wrote her history, *The Alexiad*. She despised the Crusaders though, clearly, Bohemond fascinated her. Two passages on this spread give her impressions of the First Crusade and Bohemond.

Alexius worries

When the Crusader leaders arrived at Constantinople, the Emperor Alexius greeted them courteously, showered them with gifts and entertained them lavishly. This passage, written by his daughter Anna Comnena, reveals how he really felt about them:

> **The Emperor was told about their [the Crusaders] coming and he dreaded it. He knew they were hasty and unreliable. He knew they were greedy for treasure and could not be trusted to keep treaties . . . But when the army arrived it was much worse than expected.**
>
> **(*The Alexiad*, c.1140)**

From this account, why do you think Alexius only allowed six Crusaders at a time into Constantinople?

Why would you need to treat Anna Comnena's description of the Crusaders with care?

CHECK YOUR UNDERSTANDING

Can you remember the meaning of the following?

oath
charismatic
pillage
infidel

CAN YOU REMEMBER ?

Three leaders of the First Crusade?
What Alexius's policy was towards the Crusade?
Where most of the Crusading armies came from?
Where the Fatimid Muslims held power?

Emperor Alexius.

THINGS TO DO

1 Anna Comnena's account of Bohemond depicts him as a charismatic leader.
Either: write about other leaders in the Crusades whose personality would make you want to follow them (use this book to help you).
Or: write about any famous leader from history whose strong personality won them support (use your school or local library).

2 Using the map, name three cities which Alexius would expect the Crusaders to return to him as they had promised.

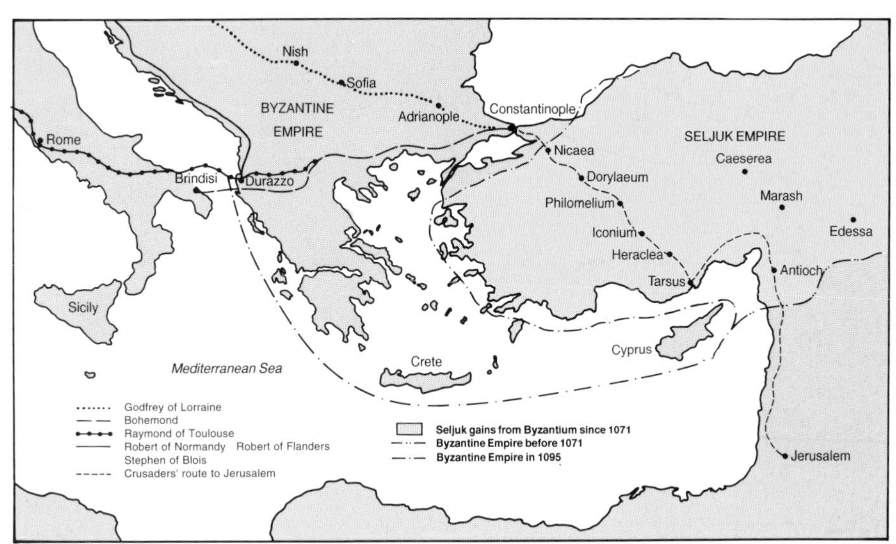

Seljuk gains from Byzantium since 1071.

Bohemond

Everyone shivered at his [Bohemond's] name. None had met a man like him before. He was more than a foot taller than anyone else. The sight of him caused astonishment, the mention of his name occasioned [created] panic. His mind ranged over all possibilities, dared anything and rushed into any undertaking... his responses were always ambiguous [with a double meaning]... His blue eyes expressed both courage and dignity... Even his laugh made his followers shiver.

(*The Alexiad*, c.1140)

What does this second source tell us about Bohemond? Do you think it shows a different person to the first source?

This account of Bohemond suggests he was a very charismatic person: someone whose personality makes them capable of influencing large numbers of other people. For example, to encourage his troops to go on the Crusade, he tore his red cloak into strips and presented pieces to his captains, who formed the strips into crosses. This next source, written by an unknown Norman soldier who went on the Crusade, gives another view of Bohemond:

> **When the emperor [Alexius] had heard that Bohemond, that most noble lord, had arrived at Constantinople, he gave orders that he should be received honourably, but also, cautiously, that he should be looked after outside the city.**
>
> **(*The Deeds of the Franks*, c.1100)**

TREACHERY AT ANTIOCH

By May 1097 the Crusaders had marched as far as Nicaea, which they besieged. Fulcher wrote that the Seljuks, 'let down hooks and seized the bodies of our wounded under the walls and the dead . . . having robbed the corpse they threw the carcass over the walls'. The Crusaders retaliated by catapulting the heads of decapitated Muslims into the city. When Alexius cut off the Seljuk food supply the garrison (defending troops) surrendered to him; but the Crusaders were disgusted at his promise to provide the prisoners with safe passage. They had another shock when Alexius also freed a nun (a survivor of Peter the Hermit's Crusade), who had been seduced by her Muslim captor. After a few days with her Christian rescuers she ran off with her Seljuk lover!

While the Byzantines resettled in Nicaea, the Crusaders continued their march. Near Dorylaeum, at a mountain pass, the Seljuk leader, Sultan Arslan, ambushed the Crusaders. Due to the discipline of Bohemond's Normans and a timely, surprise attack by Adhemar the Seljuks were routed.

After Dorylaeum the Muslims treated the Crusaders with great respect. These westerners were not a rabble like Peter the Hermit's Crusade. The Crusaders' advance through Asia Minor was helped by the chaos within the Muslim world. The Seljuk Empire, fighting with the Fatimids, had split into warring tribes, each of which was more concerned with raiding its neighbours than uniting against the threat of the Crusaders.

(Left) *The rout of Muslims at the battle of Dorylaeum meant that the Crusaders were a force to be reckoned with.*

The ruined walls of Antioch as seen by a nineteenth-century traveller.

As the Crusaders advanced, Alexius' imperial soldiers spread out to pacify the region and to garrison (defend) the towns. Ahead lay Antioch which the Crusaders reached in October. By this point only a few Byzantines, under the experienced Tacitius, remained with the Crusaders. Antioch was a fortified city of symbolic importance to Christians. Here, St Peter had founded the first bishopric (region under the authority of a bishop) after years of holding secret services in mountain caves. Here, too, was coined the word Christian.

From October 1097 to May 1098 the Crusaders achieved little against this heavily fortified city, its massive walls sectioned by 400 circular towers spaced 34 metres apart. Soon, one Crusader in seven had died of famine, and forage parties had to roam up to 160 kilometres for food. European medicine was helpless to prevent the spread of unfamiliar diseases among man and beast, and of 4,000 horses it is said that only 700 survived. The leaders gave up trying to stop soldiers deserting. Even Peter the Hermit, who had turned up, crept away. Tancred brought him back and, to save his reputation, Peter was pardoned in secret. Worse still, arguments among the Crusaders mounted as success faded.

In March 1098, a section of the walls was betrayed to Bohemond. The Crusaders swept through the lower city streets killing every Muslim they could find. But this success became a trap. High above them the fortified citadel (stronghold) held out, and news arrived of a large Muslim army under the leadership of Kerbogha marching to relieve Antioch. If caught between Kerbogha's army and the Muslim defenders in the citadel, the Crusaders' plight would be desperate.

At this news Stephen of Blois and a large number of northern French deserted, while Tacitius, the chief Byzantine adviser, suddenly left the Crusaders' camp to organize a more efficient supply system. Bohemond now threatened to leave unless the other leaders agreed to his lordship of Antioch once the citadel was taken. The leaders agreed reluctantly as they needed the Normans.

Meanwhile, when Alexius heard of the Crusaders' plight he hurried to their aid. At Philomelium Alexius halted. He was about to resume his march when Stephen of Blois arrived. He told Alexius, 'All our men are under a state of heavy siege, and I think by now they have been killed by the Seljuks. So go home as fast as you can' (From *The Letters of Stephen of Blois*).

News also came that a large Muslim army was approaching Nicaea and Constantinople unopposed from the east. Alexius was faced with a decision: to defend Constantinople or go to the aid of the Crusaders trapped at Antioch.

TREACHERY AT ANTIOCH

Stephen of Blois Deserts

The two passages below describe the feeling of the other Crusaders towards Stephen when he left for Philomelium:

> **The foolish Stephen had pretended to be laid low with a serious illness just before the capture of Antioch, and has withdrawn shamefully. We, who were shut up in Antioch lacking any help to save us, waited for him to come to our aid. But when he heard that the Turkish army was surrounding us, he was seized with a violent fear, and fled quickly with his army.**
>
> **(*The Deeds of the Franks,* c. 1100)**

> **Count Stephen left the siege . . . We all grieved at this, since he was a most noble man and strong in arms. If he had persevered (carried on), he would have shared in the joy when Antioch was handed over the next day. Instead it became a reproach for him. For to start well is of no use to anyone, unless he also ends well.**
>
> **(Fulcher of Chartres, *Chronicles of the Crusades,* 1101–27)**

Women Crusaders

During the ambush at Dorylaeum, one of Bohemond's knights praised the women who:

> **Brought up water for the fighting men and gallantly encouraged those who were fighting and defending them . . .**
>
> **(twelfth century, anonymous)**

Many women, men and even children had joined the Crusades as non-combatants (people without weapons). As the First Crusade began, Fulcher of Chartres wrote there were:

> **Many sighs and much weeping and wives who fell senseless to the ground for fear that they would never see their husbands again.**
>
> **(Fulcher of Chartres, *Chronicles of the Crusades,* 1101–1127)**

In what ways do the two accounts of Stephen's desertion differ and agree?

CHECK YOUR UNDERSTANDING

Can you remember the meaning of the following?

garrison
bishopric
citadel
treachery

However, families, the household of the princes, landowners and tenants, and even entire neighbourhoods joined the expedition. Pope Urban had discouraged women Crusaders unless they accompanied their menfolk, and women were expected to do the vital and often unattractive jobs of cooking, washing and picking fleas. However, some became fierce fighters, riding into battle and returning with severed heads of Muslims, which happened at the siege of Acre (page 30). Their fate, if captured, could be slavery or death.

How involved in the fighting are the women in the picture below?

Although most women who accompanied the Crusade did not take part in battle some became fierce fighters.

CAN YOU REMEMBER ?

Why the Crusaders' leaders agreed to Bohemond's demand to rule Antioch?
What helped the Crusaders in their march through Asia Minor?
Why Antioch was important to the Christians?
Who Tacitius was?

The Walls Betrayed to Bohemond

The Franks came to an agreement with the commander of one of Antioch's towers, a breast-plate maker called Firouz: they promised him silver and considerable wealth if he would betray the city to them. Its gates were opened, and a large number of Franks managed to get in by using ropes.

(Ibn al-Athir, 1192)

The writer of this passage, Ibn al-Athir, was a Muslim historian who lived from 1160–1233. His main work was *A Perfect History*, which filled 13 books. In this passage he talks about the 'Franks' – this was the Muslim word for all the Crusaders, whatever country they came from. Given that he is writing almost 100 years after the events in this passage, how do you think he gathered his information? Do you think there are any advantages of writing so long after the event?

THINGS TO DO

1 Either: explain in your own words the trap in which the Crusaders found themselves when Bohemond captured a section of the walls at Antioch.
Or: Draw a strip cartoon of the attack on Antioch and Stephen's desertion.
2 Ask a teacher or parent to arrange a visit to a local castle with its walls still intact. This will give you an idea of why it was so difficult for the Crusaders to capture Antioch. Look at the pictures of sieges in this book so you can compare the castles shown with the real thing.
3 What decision would you make if you were Alexius – do you protect Constantinople or go to the Crusaders' rescue?
Why were the Crusade's leaders reluctant to accept Bohemond's demands?

THE CAPTURE OF JERUSALEM

Alexius dared not ignore the threat to Constantinople. Moreover, if this Muslim army overran Nicaea and northern Asia Minor, he would be cut off from his capital. Alexius never forgot his first priority, which was to protect his Empire. Therefore, without hesitation, he marched north leaving the Crusaders to their fate. It was probably the most sensible decision; but the Crusaders couldn't understand it. To them, total commitment meant fellow Christians helping the Crusade even when it was very dangerous to do so. The Crusaders never forgave Alexius.

Bohemond was delighted at the news of Alexius's desertion. Inspired by Bohemond, and encouraged by favourable miracles such as the discovery in a church of the Holy Lance (with which it was believed a Roman had pierced Jesus's side when being led to his place of execution) the Crusaders defeated Kerbogha. At once the Muslim leader in Antioch surrendered to Bohemond who occupied the citadel. Raymond objected, but his soldiers were fought off by the Normans.

By late October 1098 Bohemond had a firm grip on Antioch which became the first principality (territory ruled by a prince) of the Crusade. When the other leaders reminded Bohemond of his solemn oath to return Antioch to Alexius, the Norman argued that Alexius's treachery released him from his promise. Before the capture of Antioch, Baldwin, the landless brother of Godfrey, had vanished east. He now returned claiming his

own county of Edessa. For some months Raymond and Godfrey dawdled, resentful of Bohemond and Baldwin, and worried about their relationship with Alexius. Adhemar might have healed the wounds but he had died of typhoid in August. Ordinary Crusaders were becoming restless at their leaders' squabbles. On 13 January 1099, Raymond left Antioch. Raymond may have been glad that Bohemond was tied to Antioch so that he could have a freer hand when the Crusaders reached Jerusalem. A month later Godfrey, Robert of Flanders and Tancred followed.

On 7 June the Crusaders camped outside the walls of Jerusalem. Discomfort, lack of food and water – the drinking wells outside the city had been poisoned and the cattle driven inside the walls – shortage of timber for building siege towers, and news of a huge Muslim army advancing quickly from Egypt to Jerusalem once more made the Crusaders lose heart. Jerusalem, now in the hands of the Seljuks, seemed indestructible. On three sides the walls plunged into deep ravines. Only from the north and a small sector in the south-west could the walls be attacked.

The Crusaders tried to smash the walls with battering rams. But the defenders lowered bales of straw between the walls and the battering rams hoping that, by absorbing the shock-waves, the bales would protect the walls from the rams. Whereupon, the Crusaders set fire to the straw. What the Crusaders needed most was timber to build siege towers. Sailors from Genoa (in Italy) broke up their ships bringing supplies, and carried the wooden planks across country to the Crusaders' camp.

(Far left) *The capture of Jerusalem by Crusader forces in 1099.*

After it fell Jerusalem was looted by the victorious crusaders.

THE CAPTURE OF JERUSALEM

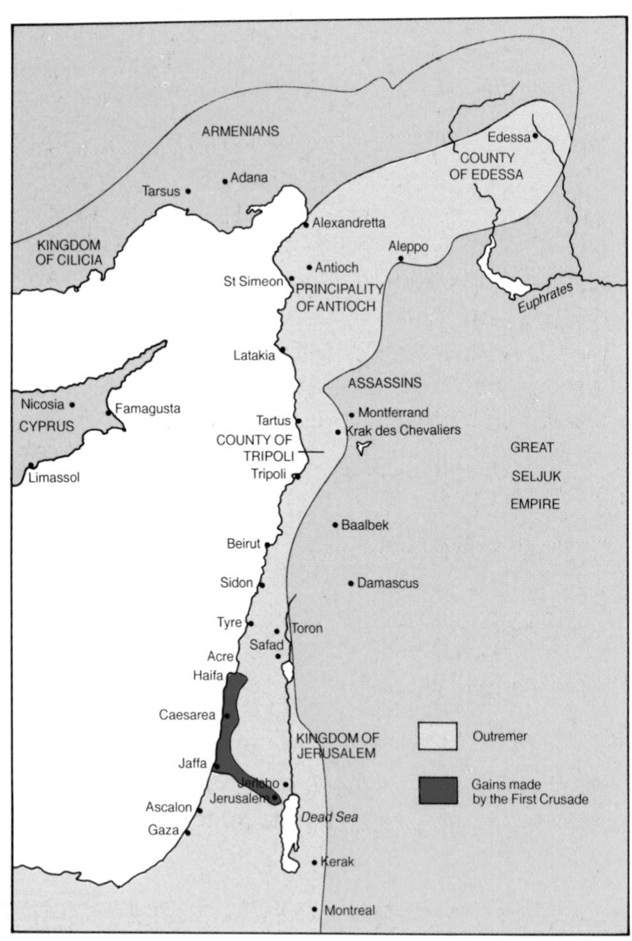

Outremer.

The Assault on Jerusalem

The following three documents describe what happened when the siege-towers were ready. The first two accounts are by eyewitnesses.

> **Count Raymond on his side, to the south, led his wooden castle near to the wall. Between the castle and the wall there was a ditch. It was given out that any soldier who carried three stones to fill the ditch should be given a penny. It took three days and nights to fill it. On 15 July, the [siege] castle was brought close to the wall. The defenders fought vigorously against our men, using great fire and stones. The Count yelled to his men, 'What are you waiting for? All the Franks are already in the town.' Once in the town our pilgrims pursued the Muslims, massacring them right up to the Temple of Solomon. Only the governor, called Iftikhar, and his household survived.**
>
> **(*The Deeds of the Franks*, c.1100)**

CHECK YOUR UNDERSTANDING

Can you remember the meaning of the following?

siege
principality
Holy Lance
battering ram

CAN YOU REMEMBER ?

Why Bohemond was glad that Alexius refused to help the Crusaders at Antioch?
Why wood was so important for the Crusaders? How they obtained it eventually?
What difficulties faced the Crusaders at the siege of Jerusalem?
What part 'visions and miracles' played in the siege?

THINGS TO DO

1 After the capture of Antioch the Crusaders had a clear idea of Alexius's policy. Either: write a report to Alexius complaining that he is betraying the Crusade.
Or: imagine you are Alexius and write a reply justifying your actions.

2 Study the picture of the siege of Jerusalem. Make a list of the methods of attack it shows the Crusaders using. Can you think of any other ways not shown?

On 15 July a knight on the Mount of Olives began to wave his shield to those who were with Count Raymond signalling them to advance. Who he was, we have been unable to discover. At his signal our men took heart and captured the wall. Our archers shot burning firebrands wrapped in cotton . . . Then the Count released the long drawbridge from the top of the tower to the city wall. It made a bridge and our men began to enter the city bravely. Among those who entered first was the Duke of Lorraine and our men shed much Turkish blood.

(Raymond of Aguilers, chaplain to Count Raymond, *History of the Franks Who Captured Jerusalem*, 1097–99)

The Franks besieged Jerusalem for more than six weeks. They built two towers, one of which, near Sion, the Turks burnt down killing everyone inside it . . . In fact the city was taken from the North on the morning of Friday, 15 July. The population was put to the sword by the Franks . . . They massacred over 70,000 men, among them scholars and devout hermits . . . They stripped the dome of the Rock of more than forty heavy silver candelabra . . . and a great deal more booty.

(Ibn al-Athir, a Muslim writing about 100 years later, see page 15)

What fact does the third source mention that the others don't? Why do you think this is?

Visions and Miracles

Many Crusaders experienced visions of saints, dreams of Jesus urging them on, odd coincidences and miracles. These were assumed to bear the stamp of heavenly approval and were very important to medieval people. They made sense of the suffering to the Christians and kept up their courage. When the Crusaders made their final attack on Jerusalem, several soldiers swore they saw the figure of Bishop Adhemar, their former Church leader, holding up a cross and beckoning to them.

On a more earthy level, the knight, Radulph of Caen, described something that happened to Tancred while he was leading a band in a desperate search for wood.

The leaders decided to inspect all the hiding places . . . to scrape together wood from everywhere for the siege-towers. Tancred had almost decided to give up the search when he was struck by dysentery [a stomach illness that causes diarrhoea] . . . While Tancred was relieving himself he faced a cave where 400 timbers lay open to view.

(*The Deeds of Tancred*, early 12th century)

What was important about Tancred's experience to the Crusaders?

LIFE IN OUTREMER

After the plunder and wholesale slaughter of the Muslims, the leaders were faced with the problem of organizing their conquests. Godfrey of Lorraine was elected King of the newly-formed Kingdom of Jerusalem, but he refused to wear the crown in the city where Christ had worn a crown of thorns. Within a year Godfrey died. He was succeeded by his younger brother, Baldwin, who was not so humble.

Baldwin rejoiced in his title, King of the Kingdom of Jerusalem. Like many poorer younger sons, Baldwin's future in Europe would have been bleak because his elder brother would have inherited everything from their father – the Crusade was therefore a golden opportunity to knights like Baldwin. Baldwin was a strong and competent king, though a chilling personality.

Europe was jubilant when news of the capture of Jerusalem reached the West. However, once the excitement faded, it was realized that the position of the Crusader settlers (called Franks or Latins by the Muslims) was precarious (not secure). Many Crusaders returned home, and the few who remained were vulnerable to Muslim aggression.

As the Crusaders settled down in the Kingdom of Jerusalem they realized that their survival depended on understanding and tolerance of Islam. Many adopted the eastern way of life.

(Right) *The remains of Caesarea, showing a typical Crusader vaulted street.*

Within a dozen years the outstanding leaders of the First Crusade had died or left. Raymond of Toulouse had founded the county of Tripoli. He was very disappointed not to be offered the crown. But he carried little authority in spite of his power, and was too friendly with Alexius to win the loyalty of the princes. Raymond died in 1105. The dashing and grasping Bohemond made his pilgrimage to Jerusalem, returned to Antioch where, raiding deep into Muslim territory, he was ambushed and captured. Ransomed in 1103, he raised a Crusade in Europe against Byzantium and was defeated. He returned to his estate in southern Italy and died in obscurity.

Of the important seaports only Jaffa and Haifa were in Crusaders' hands (see map on page 18). A narrow band of land connected the occupied seaports with Jerusalem. North lay the isolated principality of Antioch, and the states of Tripoli and Edessa, the last of which sprawled across both banks of the Euphrates. It was 40 years before these states known as Outremer were linked. Within this frontier, and beyond, existed tribes of Muslims, Christians and Jews. Among the fiercest neighbours of the Franks was a Shiite sect called Hashishiyun or the Assassins. They inhabited a string of castles along the frontier of Antioch and Tripoli. The Assassins had acquired their grim reputation by being hired to kill important people. Under the influence of their unbending religion and hashish (a dried plant taken as a drug) they took wild risks in carrying out political assassinations.

It was clear that Outremer was insecure. Inspired by the emotional success of the First Crusade, and anxious to help the Franks consolidate, waves of reinforcements left the West. Many perished in the waterless wasteland of Asia Minor. These disasters closed the overland route across Asia Minor. Immigrant Franks had to use the seaports, more of which came under Crusader control with the aid of Italian traders (pages 32 to 35) from Pisa, Genoa and Venice who were attracted by the trading prospects.

Outremer was soon organized along feudal lines which were familiar in Europe. A network of duties and responsibilities was established. For instance, the Counts of Tripoli and Edessa were vassals of the Kings of Jerusalem: that is, they promised to support and obey the Kings in return for protection and property. The Emirs (Muslim rulers) of Arsuf and Caesarea acknowledged the overlordship of Godfrey and paid tribute (tax) provided their faith and customs were honoured.

The first generation of Franks gradually realized that survival depended on understanding and tolerance (respect) of Islam. Once so bigoted towards Islam, many Franks formed alliances and truces with Emirs which, for centuries, the Byzantines had found was the best way to maintain peace and prosperity. Later Crusaders, always hostile to Islam, could never understand why the Franks would not renounce local treaties and support a new Crusade.

Despite tolerance and goodwill many Franks never forgot that they had a holy mission to destroy Islam; nor did the Muslims forget that the Crusaders were intruders or easily forgive the horror of the sack of Jerusalem in 1099. If the Crusaders had shown more restraint on that occasion, the Muslims might have accepted the Franks as another element in the already very complicated politics of Palestine. As it was, only the lack of unity within the Islamic world delayed a Muslim counter-attack.

LIFE IN OUTREMER

Despite treachery and broken truces many Crusaders adapted to the eastern way of life. The Franks soon preferred the loose, flowing Muslim robes which were better suited to the climate than heavy woollen material. King Baldwin himself wore oriental dress. Franks and Muslims traded freely with each other; friendships developed and both entertained each other at home after a day's hunting with falcons. Sometimes, inter-racial marriages took place. The Franks used soap and took baths – the dirtiness of the Europeans had always startled the more refined Muslims.

The ancient wall of Caesarea.

Peaceful Co-existence

Caesarea was a typical Crusader lordship. Surrounding the city were small estates called fiefdoms whose knights owed allegiance to the lord who, in turn, paid homage to the King of Jerusalem. The lord did not farm himself. Instead, he took one quarter to one third of the harvest from Muslim and Syrian Christian villagers. Always desperate for immigrants, the Franks granted a house and 150 acres (370 hectares) of land to any European who took the risk of settling in Palestine. New towns like Qubeiba were built to accommodate these colonists. The colonists, some of whom may have been landless peasants at home in Europe, arrived in Outremer as small property owners under the same legal system as privileged landowners. The source below and those from Usamah show how Crusaders and Muslims, who lived in hundreds of places similar to Caesarea and Qubeiba, could co-exist. A twelfth-century Muslim writer, Ibn Jubayre, wrote this as he travelled through Outremer:

> **We passed through villages and cultivated lands all inhabited by Muslims, who live in great well-being under the Franks. Our people pay less tax under the Christians. One of the chief tragedies of the Muslims is that they have to complain of injustices of their own rulers, whereas they cannot but praise the behaviour of the Franks, their natural enemies. May Allah soon put an end to this state of affairs!**
>
> **(*The Travels*, 1182–85)**

What do you think Ibn Jubayre means by 'May Allah soon put an end to this state of affairs'?

Crusader coins from Antioch. Left *Tancred (1104–12).* Right *Bohemond III (1162–1201).*

Friendships crossed religious barriers despite the wars. This picture shows a Christian and a Muslim playing chess.

Usamah's Stories of Outremer

The passages below were recorded by a Muslim historian, the aristocratic Usamah Ibn-Munqidh, who lived alongside the Franks in the twelfth century. Both passages come from his autobiography *An Arab Syrian Gentleman of the Crusades*.

A Muslim visits a Frankish friend of Usamah:

> **Some Franks have settled in our land and taken to living like Muslims. These are better than those who have just arrived from their homelands . . . I came across one in Antioch. This Frank had retired from the army and lived off the income of a property he owned. He had a fine table brought out, spread with a splendid selection of appetising food. He saw that I was not eating and said, 'Don't worry, please; eat what you like, for I don't eat Frankish food. I have Egyptian cooks. No pig's flesh ever comes into my life.'**

The tactless behaviour of a new settler is observed by Usamah:

> **When I used to enter the mosque which was occupied by the Templars (*page 28*), who were my friends, they would evacuate the little adjoining mosque so that I might pray in it. One day, one of the Franks rushed on me and turned my face eastward, saying, 'That is the way thou shouldst pray'. My friends, the Templars, remonstrated (argued in protest) with the Frank, but after it happened again, they threw him out apologizing to me, saying, 'This is a stranger who has only recently arrived from the land of the Franks and he has never seen anyone praying except eastward.'**

What do you learn from these sources about how the Crusaders and Muslims got on with each other? What does the first source tell us about the differences between Muslims and Christians?

CAN YOU REMEMBER ?

What the Assassins were famous for?
Why the Crusade benefited knights like Baldwin?
What the Franks borrowed from Islamic culture?

CHECK YOUR UNDERSTANDING

Can you remember the meaning of the following?

colonist
Outremer
emir
fiefdom
tolerance

THINGS TO DO

1 Using your school or local library, find out more about the Assassins. How do we use the word assassin today?
2 If you had returned to Europe after the First Crusade, what advice would you give the next generation of Crusaders?
3 Using a French dictionary, try to work out the meaning of Outremer.

THE MUSLIMS FIGHT BACK

During the 1120s a Muslim leader, Imad al-Din Zengi, united several Muslim states in Syria. In 1144 Zengi suddenly attacked Edessa whose count, Joscilin, was quarrelling with his neighbour, Raymond, Lord of Antioch. Edessa fell at once. No Crusader lord came to Joscilin's aid. That a Crusader estate had surrendered so easily to the first Muslim counter-attack sent shock waves through Europe, and the Second Crusade was launched.

The Second Crusade led by Conrad III, Emperor of Germany, and Louis VII, King of France, soon ran into trouble. Conrad became ill, so remained at the court of Manuel I, the Byzantine Emperor, until he regained his strength. The French, who had decided to carry on alone, were mauled (battered) by the Muslims as they struggled through Asia Minor.

Eventually, in 1148, Conrad caught up with Louis in Acre. They were joined by Baldwin III, King of Jerusalem, and many of his vassal barons. The Franks urged an attack on Damascus which was the one Muslim state anxious for friendship with the Christians. The reason for this misguided decision was the self-interest of the Franks, who hoped to use the new Crusade to grab the rich lands around Damascus. The Crusade crumbled before the walls of Damascus and the survivors drifted back to Europe in shame. A relative of Conrad admitted that the Crusade had gained nothing except, 'the salvation of many souls for much had been the suffering'.

Some historians, mainly English and Northern French writers, blame Eleanor of Aquitaine, the wife of Louis VII, for the failure of the Second Crusade because the presence of noble women like her slowed the expedition's progress as they insisted on taking their baggage and hundreds of retainers (servants) with them.

Not for 40 years would another Crusade leave the west – then terrible news reached Europe. A remarkable Muslim had succeeded Zengi's heirs. His name was Saladin. By 1175 Saladin had united the Muslim world from the Upper Nile river to northern Iraq.

While the Seljuks revived under Saladin's inspiration, Outremer was in crisis. The heir to King Amalric of Jerusalem was the nine-year-old Baldwin. One day the boy's tutor noticed that, while playing with his friends, Baldwin felt no pain when he bled from cuts. The tutor suspected, correctly, that the boy had leprosy. Not only did Baldwin die young but so did his successor. After a bitter struggle for the throne, Guy of Lusignan seized the crown.

While the Franks wrangled over the succession, Saladin closed in on Outremer. In 1187, at the Horns of Hattin which overlooked the Sea of Galilee, Saladin destroyed the finest army that the Franks had ever assembled. Wood, thought to be the Holy Cross on which Christ died, was captured

Saladin and Richard I in combat. The English artist optimistically shows Saladin being defeated.

when the Bishop of Acre was killed. King Guy was taken prisoner, and many knights captured or killed. The Kingdom of Jerusalem was leaderless; and Outremer was defenceless. Most of the kingdom was overrun. On 2 October, Jerusalem surrendered to Saladin. Of the important seaports only Tyre and Tripoli held out. Europe was stunned and Pope Urban III died, perhaps of grief.

In 1190 the Third Crusade, called 'The Crusade of the Kings', assembled under the joint (and often argumentative) leadership of the three strongest monarchs of the time: Richard I (Coeur de Lion), King of England, Philip of France and Frederick, Emperor of Germany. Frederick was drowned early on, and after Richard and Philip captured Acre (page 30), Philip returned home where he stirred up trouble in Richard's French lands. Richard won important victories at Arsuf and Jaffa, but failed to recapture Jerusalem. Saladin could no more drive the Crusaders out of Palestine than Richard could take Jerusalem. On this understanding, which recognized the limitations of the Crusading movement, the leaders agreed to a five year truce, in 1192. The Crusaders controlled several seaports and a ten mile strip of coastline from Jaffa to Tyre, yet Jerusalem remained in Muslim hands. Nonetheless, Saladin assured safe passage for pilgrims to the Holy City and freedom for Christians to worship there. He also encouraged minority groups like Jews to return to Jerusalem.

Soon after, Richard left Palestine to re-assert his authority in England where his brother, John, was rebelling. On his way home he was imprisoned by the Duke of Austria whom Richard had insulted at Acre. Ransomed in 1194, Richard spent his last years fighting Philip in France where he died in 1199 from a chance shot by a crossbowman.

Soldiers who were captured were often ransomed or sold as slaves. Both sides sometimes executed prisoners in revenge. Here Christian prisoners await execution.

THE MUSLIMS FIGHT BACK

Saladin

Saladin, whose full name was Salah ad-Din Yusuf Ibn Ayyub, was born into a Kurdish military family. Muslim and Christian alike agreed that Saladin was an honourable man, and the most attractive figure of the crusading times.

Sometimes Saladin could be severe. After the Battle of Hattin, among the Christian prisoners were a number of the Knights of the Templars and Hospitallers (page 28). Such was the awe and fear which these dedicated 'Fighting Monks' inspired in the Muslims that Saladin dared not spare their lives. Each one was beheaded.

In contrast, when Jerusalem surrendered, Saladin allowed the survivors to buy their freedom. Many poorer people couldn't, so Saladin lowered the price.

Saladin died in 1193. Though criticized by Muslims for failing to destroy Outremer, his reputation has survived. The following extracts give us impressions of Saladin. A doctor from Baghdad, Abdal-Latif, wrote in the 12th century:

> **I found him [Saladin] a great prince whose appearance inspired at once respect and love, who was approachable, deeply thoughtful, and noble in his thoughts. All who came near him took him as their model. I found him surrounded by a huge assembly of learned men who were discussing various sciences. He listened with pleasure and his talk was full of clever ideas.**

When Jerusalem fell to Saladin, Ambrose, a monk and admirer of Richard I, wrote:

> **When Saladin took Jerusalem he found in the city two ancient men . . . They asked him to let them stay and end their lives in Jerusalem. He gladly granted this and ordered that they should be given what they needed, as much as they needed.**
>
> **(*The History of the Holy War*, 1190–2)**

An unknown canon (church official) in London wrote about Saladin in a book on Richard I in the early 13th century:

> **Saladin made a disgraceful income out of the prostitutes of Damascus. None of them could carry on her filthy trade without first buying a licence from him. He spent the money on entertainers. That king of the brothels, who fought in the taverns, and spent his time gambling.**
>
> **He conquered countries either by trickery or force. But the greedy tyrant concentrated all his efforts on an attempt to seize the Holy Land, Palestine.**

A Muslim, Baha' ad-Din ibn Shaddad, travelled with Saladin and wrote a biography on him in the 12th century:

> **Saladin did not spend a single gold or silver coin on anything except jihad [holy war]. Out of his desire to fight for God's cause he left behind his family, children, country, home and all the towns under his control.**

Compare these accounts. How could you use them to (a) praise or (b) criticize Saladin?

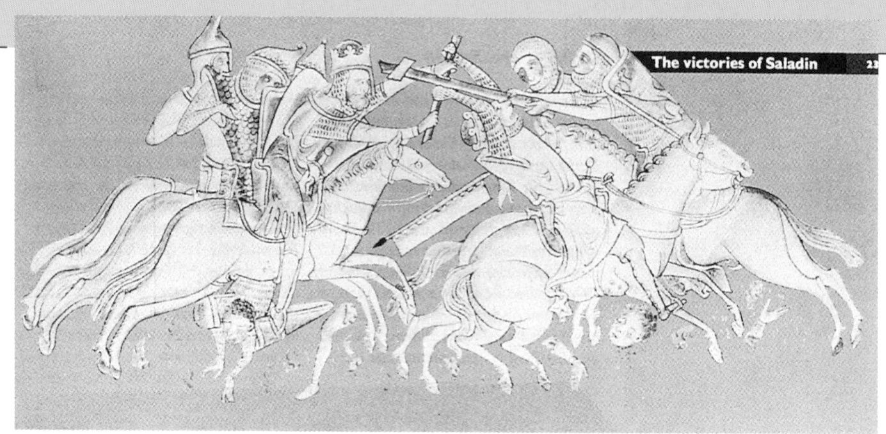

Richard I.

Richard I And Saladin

When Richard (who had a fever) and Saladin were negotiating peace, Saladin sent peaches and snow from Mount Herman to cool Richard's drink. Though it is unlikely that the two leaders ever met in person, an unknown English churchman in the early 1200s described Richard's parting words:

> **. . . he Richard would return and wrest the whole territory of Jerusalem from Saladin's grasp . . . Saladin thought Richard so pleasant, upright and excellent that he would rather have it taken into Richard's mighty power than have it go into the hands of any other prince whom he had ever seen.**
>
> **(*The Journey of King Richard*, possibly based on the writing of Monk Ambrose, c.1205)**

CHECK YOUR UNDERSTANDING

Can you remember the meaning of the following?

patriarch	mauled
retainers	vassal

CAN YOU REMEMBER ?

What mistake the leaders of the Second Crusade made?
What happened at the Horns of Hattin?
What agreement Richard I and Saladin reached in 1192?

THINGS TO DO

1 With a friend, write a dialogue (conversation) between Richard and Saladin, each of you writing one part. Perhaps you could imagine that you met after the Third Crusade ended and discussed your hopes and disappointments. Information in the next chapter will help you.

2 Look at the two pictures of Saladin. Do you think the artists have painted Saladin's armour correctly?

The loss of the True Cross by the Crusader army at the battle of Hattin.

Saladin imaginatively portrayed by a European artist.

THE FIGHTING MONKS

Maintaining a regular army was always as difficult for the Franks as it was for the Muslims. Most soldiers were farmers and preferred to fight when their crops had been sown or harvested. In both armies mercenaries were used who were likely to disappear after they had completed their contract, if not before. Some kind of permanent army was necessary which, at a moment's notice, would be ready to defend Outremer and to protect pilgrims.

Out of this need a knight called Hugh of Payens and eight friends founded the Military Order of the Knights Templar, so called because King Baldwin accommodated them in the Royal Palace in the Temple enclosure of Jerusalem. The Hospitallers (or Knights of St John of the Hospital) joined the Templars in defending the Kingdom of Jerusalem. Both Orders were drawn from the élite of noble families. They acquired the name 'Fighting Monks' because they combined the strict monastic vows of poverty and obedience with the discipline of formidable warriors. Such was their religious zeal (enthusiasm) that at their execution after Hattin (page 24), they crowded and jostled each other to seize the privilege of being the first to die. At Cresson, in 1187, just three Templars survived when 300 knights went into battle against 7000 Muslims.

The Hospitallers were famous, too, for running hospitals where patients had a bed each, instead of sharing, and fresh meat. In Jerusalem, there were 2000 beds and a ward for babies born to pilgrims. On the battlefield the Hospitallers tended the wounded after fighting. They carried a dagger with a slender blade which could be slipped through narrow joints of armour into the body of those who could not be saved.

The Military Orders only had 600 knights between them at any one time in Outremer, but they established a network of monasteries and staff all over Europe. In London, you can still see the Temple Church which was first built in 1185.

Despite their simple lifestyle the Knights became as rich and powerful as modern global corporations. They owned 40 per cent of Outremer and were bankers to the Kings of France and England. By the 13th century the Templars were financing crusades which led them into the shipping business. Pilgrims and crusaders preferred to sail to Palestine under the arrangements of the Templars whom they could

The Crusaders besieged Acre for over two years. It finally fell when Richard I arrived to help King Guy of Jerusalem.

(Left) *A Muslim slave market. Captives were often sold as slaves.*

trust, unlike other entrepreneurs (enterprising businessmen) who might land their passengers in Muslim slave markets. Even some Muslims entrusted the Templars with their money affairs.

Yet the Military Orders never lost sight of their aim to defend Outremer. They built a string of impressive castles, often clinging to giddy precipices. These formed the defensive network of Outremer as well as commanding the caravan trade routes.

When Outremer finally fell to the Muslims in 1291, the Templars were among the last to leave. At the fall of Acre, the Templars fought to the last amid the destruction of their collapsing castle – many of them were buried in the rubble.

After a scandal during which the Templars were accused of lurid (terrible) crimes, Philip IV of France suppressed the Order in 1311 and, having taken over their assets (income), handed their estates to the Hospitallers. Many Templars, the 'fiery heart' of the crusaders as the Muslims called them, were publicly burnt alive. The Pope, to whom the Military Orders were accountable, was helpless to prevent Philip's savage action against an Order whose greatest offence, perhaps, was to become richer and more powerful than the King.

THE FIGHTING MONKS

In battle the Crusaders depended on heavily armoured knights who thundered into the attack hoping to crush and scatter the opposition. The Muslims' main fighting group was also their horsemen but they were much lighter armed, more mobile and their offensive weapon was the arrow. The Muslims were skilled mounted archers, firing from the saddle at full speed and, alarmingly, from the horse's flank when riding away. The Muslims avoided frontal attacks until the Crusader ranks had become thinned or disorganized through casualties or exhaustion. Provided the Crusaders could withstand the early rain of missiles, which seemed to blot out the sun, their charge could be decisive, as at Richard's victories at Arsuf and Jaffa.

Seljuk Tactics

Typical Seljuk tactics are described by an unknown writer who travelled with Richard's army from Acre to Jerusalem.

> **The Seljuks are not weighed down with armour like our men. They carry only a bow, a club with sharp teeth, a sword, a lance and knife. When defeated they flee away on the swiftest horses, but when they see their pursuers slacken, they return like a persistent fly which, though you drive it off, will return directly you stop your efforts. It is just like that with the Seljuk. When you stop trying to catch him, he returns to worry you.**
>
> **(*The Journey of King Richard*, c.1205)**

The Siege of Acre (1191)

Most castles could withstand sieges for a long time. Usually, surrender came through famine, treachery, or the failure of a relief army to arrive in time. Very few castles or fortified towns were taken by arms. Surprisingly, the siege of Acre by the Crusaders was an exception.

Acre had been under siege for two years when Richard I arrived in 1191. Richard had destroyed some Muslim relief ships and was able to blockade Acre by sea, while on the land side the Crusaders sealed off the city from behind their own ramparts. Beyond, they were overlooked by Saladin's army. The following accounts tell us what happened.

Standard bearers from the Muslim forces.

CAN YOU REMEMBER ?

Why the Military Orders were needed?
The three most likely ways a castle would be captured?
The nickname for the Military Orders?
How the Seljuks used to fight?

Aerial view of Krak des Chevaliers, the Hospitaller castle which was one of the greatest in Christendom. It can still be seen in modern-day Syria.

From his bed he [Richard] shot many of the enemy by his own skill with the arbalest [crossbow]. In addition his sappers [engineers] carried a mine under the tower, filled it with logs of wood and set them on fire [this caused the masonry to splinter]. A trebuchet [stone-throwing catapult] also hurled frequent blows at the tower, a part of which collapsed with a great crash . . . Then Richard offered four gold pieces for each stone removed . . . our knights under the Bishop of Salisbury rode into the city . . . There still remained 6000 Turks, but they were now in need of reinforcements . . .

(Monk Ambrose, *The History of the Holy War*, 1190–92)

The story now moves to Saladin's camp.

A letter arrived from the beleaguered garrison. 'We have reached a pitch of exhaustion. We can do nothing but surrender. Tomorrow, if you can do nothing for us, we shall beg for our lives and hand over the city.' Saladin tried, by assault, to re-establish contact with his garrison. But the enemy infantry stood firm, like an unbeatable wall, with weapons, ballisters [large crossbows] and arrows, behind their bastions [defences]. We could not get through.

(From Beha ed-Din, who entered Saladin's service in 1188 and was a close adviser at Acre)

Using the above extracts on the siege of Acre, give four reasons why the Crusaders were able to capture the city.

CHECK YOUR UNDERSTANDING

Can you remember the meaning of the following?

entrepreneurs blockade
assets trebuchet

THINGS TO DO

1 When next on a history field trip, take an area of land and decide either: where you would put a castle so that it was in the best defensive position. or: decide the best place for an ambush using fast mounted troops like the Seljuks. Give reasons for your decisions.
2 You have just joined the Templars. Write a letter to a knight you know in France telling him why you joined the Military Orders in Outremer.
3 Today's St John Ambulance Brigade is a modern descendant of the Hospitallers, the Knights of the Hospital of St John of Jerusalem. Find out what you can about this organization and compare it with the ideals of the Hospitallers.

ITALIAN TRADERS

Before the Crusades, the Italian city-states of Venice, Genoa and, to a lesser extent, Pisa had traded in the Middle East. Alexandria in Egypt was the commercial centre, so the Italian cities had to be wary not to upset their trade arrangements with Muslim Egypt by supporting the Crusades too openly. On the other hand trade restrictions would hurt Muslim and Christian alike.

For the first fifty years trade was quiet in Outremer. Though states like Venice were interested in creating new trading bases, commerce was never a primary motive for the Crusades. Until about 1150 European travellers to Palestine sailed in Venetian or Genoese ships to Constantinople, and from there to Syria in Greek ships. A Genoese international lawyer, called Scriba, recorded that in the mid-12th century twice as many of his clients had interests in Alexandria as in Outremer.

Venice had a very lucrative trade with Egypt in timber and metal, which were likely to be turned into weapons and used against the very Crusaders whom the Venetians shipped increasingly to Palestine. Genoa led the market in selling slaves. These doubtful trade practices were frowned on by successive Popes who could do little apart from voice their disapproval, especially as the High Court in Acre had issued trade licences to both cities.

The Italian traders became influential when they helped the Franks capture several important seaports in Palestine. These ports were the safest entry to the Holy Land once the Asia Minor overland route had become too hazardous. The Italians made a lot of money out of transporting soldiers, diplomats and pilgrims to Palestine. From the income, the traders bought Muslim commodities cheaply and sold them as luxuries in Europe. One of the most commercially stable periods was the ten years after Saladin's recapture of Jerusalem (1187–97). United and prosperous, the Muslim caravans carried goods from Damascus and beyond to the Christian seaports where the Muslims were greeted courteously. They worshipped at their Mosque in peace and lodged in safety with Christians.

Acre was the best port for Damascus. During the years of the Crusades, Acre, the 'Constantinople of Outremer', became the most prosperous city in Outremer. It was the safest of the Palestinian seaports with two harbours. A chain separated the two harbours which was raised when customs officials had cleared and taxed the commodities (goods). A Muslim traveller, Ibn Jubayr, remarked on the safety of the caravan route from Damascus to Acre during Saladin's rule, and on the efficiency of the customs officials.

It was this trade passing through Acre which was exploited by the Italian traders. The most important commodity made in Outremer was sugar which supplied most of European demand. Otherwise, the Franks grew enough crops and fruit for themselves, though in bad harvests they had to import corn from the Muslims. The three Italian cities were allocated their own district in Acre with warehouses, markets and palaces. Within their districts the city merchants governed themselves.

A convoy took three weeks to reach Acre from Italy. Sometimes as many as 100 ships would arrive with thousands of passengers and tonnes of cargo.

Church bells pealed as the ships approached; the citizens flocked to the harbour; porters and custom officials would carry and check the goods. In the market-place products were bought and sold. Eventually, the ships returned loaded with eastern commodities.

Outremer never became as rich as the Italian traders did. There were outward signs of wealth which impressed visitors such as the Franks' adoption of Muslim silk materials, food and architectural features, but these were acquired locally and cheaply. The Kings of Jerusalem took 10 per cent of the value of commodities which were becoming fashionable in Europe, such as silk, porcelain, spices, dyes and scented wood. But a high proportion of this revenue was spent on their subjects, the Church or the Military Orders. The richest barons were the Ibelins of Beirut, who owned the nearby iron mines, and the Montforts who ran the sugar factories in Tyre ('sugar', like 'sherbert' and 'spinach', was originally an Arabic word).

Rivalry between the Italian traders was always keen, at times violent, and on occasions divided the loyalties of the barons and the interests of Outremer. When the Mongols burst on the scene in 1242 the Venetians urged the leadership in Outremer to back the new Muslim power in the Middle East, the Egyptian-based Mamluks, because Venice resented the Genoese who were doing well out of the Mongols. And when the exiled Byzantines in Nicaea plotted to regain Constantinople in 1261, they could count on Genoa's support because Venice had a virtual stranglehold on Constantinople where over 20,000 Venetians prospered. These feuds weakened Outremer at a time when unity was essential if the kingdom was to survive.

Aerial view of modern-day Acre.

New Crusaders constantly arrived from Europe.

ITALIAN TRADERS

An Expensive Venture

Louis IX, who later was made a saint, led a huge Crusade in 1248, including 2800 knights and 1800 ships which were supplied from Cyprus by Genoa. The overall cost of the Crusade was estimated to be 1,537,570 pounds, a very expensive operation given that Louis's average annual income was only about 250,000 pounds a year (the pounds here are actually *livres tournois*, pounds struck in the mint at Tours in France where the king was also the local count). In fact the French church ended up paying for almost two thirds of the total costs of the five year expedition. The list below gives some of the king's costs for part of the Crusade:

Royal Household	**£**
Food	31,595
Gifts of robes and silver	771
Crossbowmen & sergeants-at-arms	4,494
115 Warhorses, pack-horses & mules	1,916
War & Shipping	
Pay of knights	57,093
Replacement for 264 warhorses	6,789
Carpenters, engineers & other labourers	689
Spent on shipping	5,725
Ransoms	967

(From the *Royal Accounts of Louis IX*, 1252)

Do you think Genoa did well out of the shipping deal with Louis IX? Why should Louis have to budget for ransoms?

CAN YOU REMEMBER ?

The most important commercial city in the Middle East to the Franks?
The most profitable goods sold by Venice and Genoa?
Why the Italian traders had to be careful in supporting the Crusades too openly?
Why the Popes disapproved of the Italian traders?

THINGS TO DO

1 Using the modern plan of Acre, identify the quarters colonized by Venice, Genoa and Pisa on the medieval map. Write them in. Which Italian traders had the best and worst positions in the city?
2 Imagine you are a Muslim trader. Write a letter home describing the activities in Acre on a busy market day.

CHECK YOUR UNDERSTANDING

Can you remember the meaning of the following?

khan	commodities
Genoese	Asia Minor

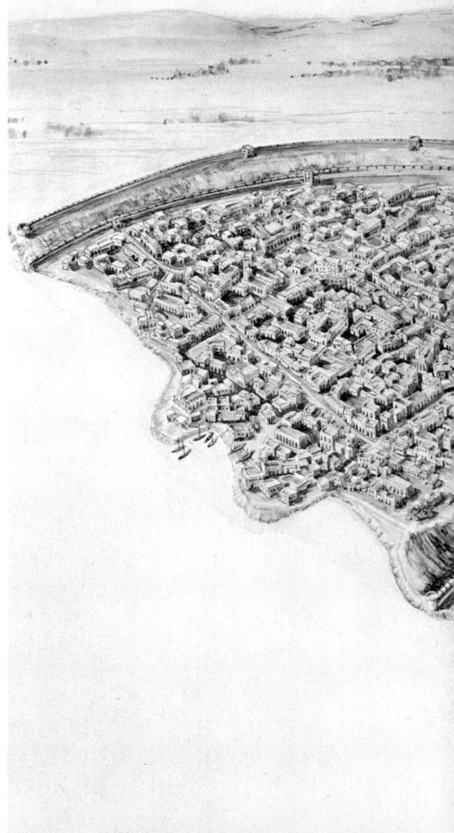

The twelfth-century Crusader sea walls at Acre.

A reconstruction of the city of Acre in the thirteenth century.

Disputes between Traders

One of the most violent feuds was fought in 1256 over a monastery in Acre which separated the Genoese and Venetian districts, which is described here by the modern historian Steven Runciman.

> **Both colonies claimed the ancient monastery of St. Sabas; while lawyers disputed the case, the Genoese took possession of it and, on the Venetians protesting, rushed armed men into the Venetian quarter. The Pisans hurried to join them; and the Venetians, taken by surprise, saw their homes sacked together with their ships at the quay.**
>
> **(*The History of The Crusades, Vol 3 The Kingdom of Acre,* 1954)**

Later, Pisa deserted Genoa. The Genoese overran the Pisan quarter. Street fighting followed when a Venetian fleet smashed the harbour cable and landed soldiers in the city. This feud spread throughout Outremer. The Templars supported Venice, the Hospitallers sided with Genoa, while the barons were divided according to their commercial interests or family connections.

Customs at Acre

Ibn Jubayr observed the custom officials of Acre at work in the late twelfth century,

> **We were taken to the custom house, which is a khan [an inn with courtyard] prepared to accommodate the caravans. Before the door are stone benches, spread with carpets, [behind] which are the Christian clerks. The baggage of any who had no merchandise was also examined in case it concealed merchandise, after which the owner was permitted to go his way.**
>
> **(*The Travels,* 1182–85)**

THE FOURTH CRUSADE

In April 1204, Pope Innocent III received news that Constantinople had been sacked by the Crusaders. In three days of unbridled destruction the Crusaders destroyed the best part of six centuries of one of the finest collections of art and craft ever assembled in a European city. All thoughts of marching on Jerusalem had been abandoned.

It may seem strange that a Crusade should end by destroying the very Christian Empire which it was supposed to be defending against Islam. Some historians believe this outrage was deliberate; after all, many Crusaders remembered how, since the days of Alexius, Byzantium had not only been lukewarm in supporting the Crusaders but had often co-operated with Muslim forces. Other historians argue that it was a dreadful mistake, and the real culprit was the rich and grasping Republic of Venice.

The Crusade's leaders were Count Boniface of Montferrat and Philip of Swabia, heir to the German throne, who both hated Byzantium. They decided to advance on the Holy Land from the south, having first subdued Egypt. Unfortunately, they had no ships. The Crusaders agreed to pay Venice 85,000 silver marks for transporting them to Egypt and feeding, for a year, 74,000 soldiers of whom 4,500 were knights. Also, 50 galleons would accompany the Crusaders on condition that half the Crusade's conquests would be given to Venice.

At the time the agreement was being signed, Venice was secretly reassuring Egypt that Venice, which had important trade facilities there, had no intention of shipping the Crusaders to Egypt. Behind this murky deal was Enrico Dandolo, the Doge ('president') of Venice. Dandolo bore several grievances against Byzantium. Years before, he had lost an eye in a street brawl in Constantinople; recently, Byzantium had reluctantly renewed a trade agreement with Venice and the Doge was worried about the insecurity of his trading position with the Empire.

Four bronze horses from the Hippodrome in Constantinople looted in 1198 can be seen in this medieval picture of Venice. (They are above the porch of St Mark's Cathedral in the top left corner.)

Pope Innocent III.

When the Crusaders could not pay the bill, Venice refused to release the ships. Burdened by this enormous debt, pestered by trade creditors who threatened to cut off their food, confined to the Lido island off Venice, not able to afford to stay or to leave, the Crusaders were in a hopeless mess. Next, Dandolo offered to extend the payment deadline if the Crusaders helped Venice to capture the harmless, Christian city of Zara in Dalmatia which Venice had long coveted (wanted to own). Yet even after Zara was captured the Crusaders still could not pay. The expedition seemed doomed before it had begun.

Then, Alexius IV, son of the deposed (forcibly removed from the throne) Byzantine Emperor Isaac Angelus, came up with an extraordinary proposal. If the Crusaders helped Alexius regain the throne of Byzantium, which had been usurped (seized unlawfully) he would pay them enough to settle their debt to Venice and to travel to Palestine. Moreover, the empire would be divided equally between Venice, the Crusaders and Alexius. And 10,000 Byzantine soldiers would join the Crusade.

To the hesitant and doubting Crusaders who were uneasy or confused by Alexius's wonderful promises, Dandolo offered bribes. Alexius assured the Crusaders that the usurper, who ruled by extortion (forcing money out of his citizens), was so unpopular that the Empire would welcome them. Apart from the material attractions, here was a Byzantine Emperor who, for the first time, promised to unite his people behind a Crusade. A few Crusaders were deeply unhappy at this idea and made their own way to Palestine. But most put to one side the contradiction that the best way to defeat Islam was, apparently, to suppress their fellow Christians in Byzantium. The Eastern Christian Empire was now in greater peril than Islam had threatened for years.

Alexius and his father were restored to the throne but were subsequently murdered. Their successor, Alexius V, did not honour the agreement. Impatient at the obstruction of the Byzantines, Boniface ordered the assault. Within a week, the Crusaders had stormed the walls and a rampage which shocked Muslims and shamed Christians followed.

Byzantium, the protector of Christianity, was broken up and divided between the Crusaders and Venice. A French count, Baldwin, was enthroned. The surviving Byzantines emigrated to Nicaea where an Imperial court in exile was established. They returned to Constantinople in 1261 on the collapse of the short-lived Frankish Empire which, by then, had alienated (made hostile) the Byzantine Greek subjects.

THE FOURTH CRUSADE

Pope Innocent III

Innocent III, trained as a lawyer, was one of the most distinguished medieval Popes. In the absence of kings, Innocent took over the Crusade's destiny of which he lost control. While genuinely shocked at the attack on Zara, he forgave the Crusaders once he heard how Venice had trapped them.

As for the capture and sack of Constantinople, it should be remembered that the Popes had always resented the refusal of the Eastern Church, linked closely to the Byzantine Empire, to recognize them as the leaders of Christendom. While Innocent III deplored the attacks on Christians, arguably he had achieved a long-established, if private, aim of the papacy in the capture of Constantinople. The extract below is from Innocent's letter to the leaders of the Crusade:

> **Therefore, none of you should rashly flatter yourself that it is acceptable for you to seize or plunder Byzantine lands on grounds that it has a lesser allegiance [loyalty] to the Apostolic See [the Pope in Rome]. It is not for you to sit in judgement on their offences. Instead, give up these pointless diversions; cross over to save the Holy Land . . . if you delay in Byzantine territory, we cannot promise you the remission [forgiveness] of sins.**
>
> **(*Letter VII, Volume CCXV*, 1204)**

What is the Pope urging the Crusaders to do? What criticism of Byzantium is the Pope making?

Alexius's Offer

Geoffrey of Villehardouin accompanied the Fourth Crusade. Here he describes the Crusaders' reaction to the tempting offer of Alexius.

> **So there was discord in the army. Nor can you wonder if the laymen [non-church people] were in disagreement, when the Cistercians [an order of monks] were equally at odds with each other. The Abbot of Vaux declared he would never give his consent, since it would mean marching against Christians. The Abbot of Loos, admired for his goodness and wisdom, preached to the troops, earnestly encouraging them to keep the army together, and accept the proposed agreement . . . At this juncture the Marquis de Montferrat, Count Louis de Blois, intervened in the dispute to announce that they intended to accept the agreement, since they would be shamed if they rejected it.**
>
> **(*The Conquest of Constantinople* c. 1208)**

Why wouldn't the Bishop of Vaux agree to Alexius's proposal?

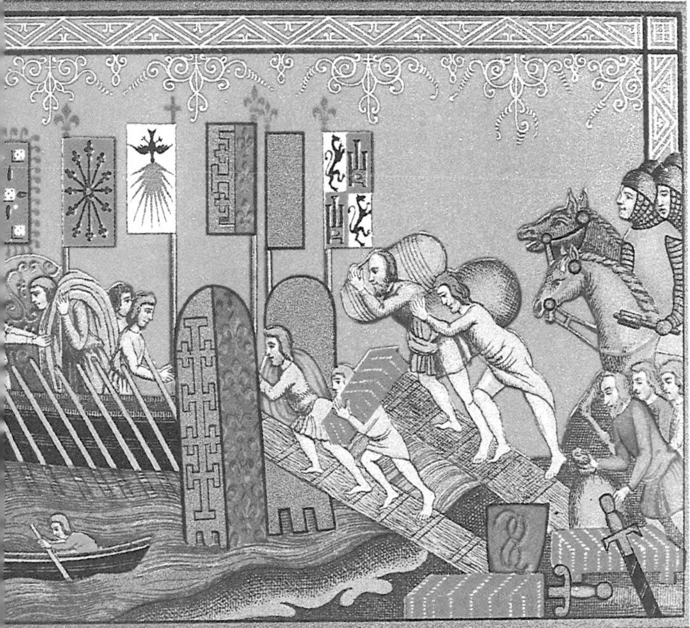

Supplies being loaded for the Crusades.

The Siege of Constantinople

Villehardouin describes how the Crusaders captured Constantinople in these extracts from *The Conquest of Constantinople*, written c. 1208.

> **This time they would have the ships that carried the scaling ladders bound together, two by two, so that each pair could make a combined attack on one tower. Two of the ships which were bound together approached so close to a tower, one of them on one side and one on the other, that the ladder of one ship made contact with the tower. Immediately, a Venetian (and a French knight) forced their way in. Other men began to follow them, and in the end the defenders were routed. Then all the rest of the troops started to leap out of warships. They broke down about three of the gates and entered the city . . . Then followed a scene of massacre and pillage: on every hand the Greeks were cut down, their horses and other possessions snatched as booty. So great was the number of killed and wounded that no one could count them.**

THINGS TO DO

1 Write a letter to Pope Innocent III explaining why you decided to join the band of Crusaders who made their own way to Palestine.
2 Make a large copy of one of the ships shown in the picture above. Then list all the things Crusading knights might need to take with them on a long voyage and indicate on your drawing the best place to store each item.

What was the point of having some of the ships tied together in pairs?

CAN YOU REMEMBER ?

The name of the Doge of Venice?
Where the Byzantine court re-established itself?
The name of the city the Crusaders attacked on Venice's behalf?
What race most Byzantine people were?

CHECK YOUR UNDERSTANDING

Can you remember the meaning of the following?

Doge
usurp
extortion
laymen

THE END OF OUTREMER

Two hundred years after Pope Urban had preached the First Crusade, Outremer ceased to exist. Crusades were organized for several hundred more years, but there was no lasting achievement.

In 1212 the Children's Crusade set out under a shepherd boy called Stephen who had been inspired by a 'vision'. Huge numbers were attracted to Stephen's expedition. The children had hoped that the Mediterranean Sea would divide allowing them to walk to Palestine, in much the same way that Moses had led his people through the Red Sea. Some children went home, the rest were offered a free passage by two devious merchants, Hugh the Iron and William the Pig, who sold them as slaves to the Muslims.

(Far right) *Edward I of England went on a Crusade to the Holy Land in 1270.*

Much of what we know about the Crusades comes from accounts written at the time. William of Tyre was one of the best-informed authors who wrote his account between 1169 and 1173.

Emperor Frederick II of Hohenstaufen did regain Jerusalem by diplomacy in 1229. However, he was blamed by Christians for not taking the Holy City with the sword, and by the Muslims for winning a diplomatic victory with their own people. For twenty years Jerusalem was an 'open city' before the Muslims re-conquered it.

After the Fourth Crusade, disillusionment in the Crusades set in. Though St Louis attempted to revive crusading in France (see page 42) a counter-Crusade movement emerged. People protested that the Crusades had been a waste; and had been responsible for more indignities, more deaths of Christians by Christians than of Muslims. Rutebruf, the French poet of the people, urged men to resist crusading.

The word 'Crusade' became discredited. Kings sought Papal blessing to attach 'Crusade' to campaigns aimed at Christian rivals. As late as the fifteenth century the Teutonic Knights won the Pope's approval to link their aggressive schemes in north-east Europe with a 'Crusade.' The Popes themselves used 'Crusades' in their endless struggles to suppress the German Emperors and the Albigensians, a heretic movement based in Albi in south-east France (1209–29). (Heretics are people whose beliefs are thought to be contrary to the official beliefs of a religious organization such as the Roman Catholic Church). Many a false cause was sustained by the magic of a 'Crusade'.

By the early fifteenth century the Muslims, now under the brilliant Osman, who founded the Ottoman Empire, were camped on the banks of the Danube, and Constantinople was surrounded. In vain, the Byzantines appealed for concerted action from the European kings. But England and France were far too busy fighting out the Hundred Years War, which ended in 1451 when France clawed back the last English-occupied land that had been the inheritance of Henry II and his queen, Eleanor.

In 1453, Constantinople fell by storm after a heroic defence. The last Byzantine Emperor, Constantine XI, rode to his death into a band of Muslims with his last words, 'The city is taken; and should I still live?'

Though the capture of Jerusalem, the principal objective of Pope Urban's appeal, was only achieved for a limited period following the First Crusade, the Crusades did bring many important Muslim discoveries to Europe, such as medical knowledge and architecture. The concentric pattern used in Muslim castle design was used as a model by Edward I when he conquered Wales – Beaumaris Castle is one striking example. Another important gain for the West was the convenient Arabic numbering system which was adopted and has been used ever since. More than this, the Crusaders who settled in Palestine learnt to tolerate people of very different beliefs and language (see pages 20 to 23).

THE END OF OUTREMER

Louis IX's Crusade

St Louis, King of France (Louis IX), was one of the few Crusading leaders whose reputation was enhanced in spite of the failure of the Fifth Crusade which he led in 1248 (see page 34 for details of his expenses). His simple life-style, piety, honour and fortitude and personal bravery were admired by Christians and Muslims. When ransomed in 1250 he refused to leave for home until the last prisoner had been freed under the same agreement with the Muslims. Louis waited four years.

Against the advice of many, including his friend and biographer John, Lord of Joinville, Louis insisted on setting out for another Crusade 20 years later. By then a sick and frail man, to whom riding was agony, he died in Tunis in 1270.

In this extract from *The Life of St Louis* (written c.1297) Joinville quotes from King Louis's advice in the late 1260s to his son and successor,

Love and honour all persons in the Service of Holy Church [Catholic Church] and see that no one takes away or diminishes the gifts and donations made to them by your predecessors. It is related [told] of King Philip, my grandfather, that one of his councillors once said to him that the servants of Holy Church were doing him much wrong and injury, in that they deprived him of his rights and trespassed on his authority, and that it was a great marvel that he allowed it to do so. The good king answered that after considering the benefits God had bestowed and His many gracious acts of kindness, he thought it better to forego some of his rights than embark on any dispute with the people of Holy Church.

Find the evidence in this book which explains why Crusading was so important to medieval people.
What does Louis's advice to his son tell us about the power of the Medieval Church?

Beaumaris Castle was built by Edward I – one of many castles that he erected to control Wales. Its design was greatly influenced by castles built in the Holy Land.

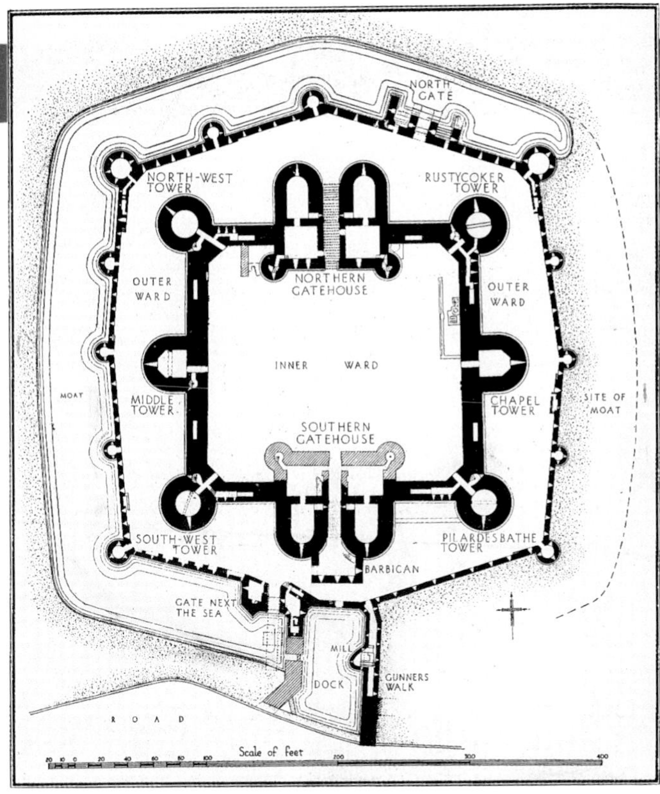

Plan of Beaumaris Castle.

Pope Pius's Plea

By 1462, the Crusading movement was virtually exhausted, as you can see by this despairing speech of Pope Pius II to six cardinals.

> **If we send ambassadors to ask the kings for their help, they are just ridiculed. If we grant indulgences (special privileges) and invite them by means of spiritual gifts to give us money, then we are accused of greed. Our sole aim is thought to be the acquisition of gold. No one believes what we say; we are left without credit, like businessmen who let down their creditors. In 1453, Philip, Duke of Burgundy, publicly made a vow to God that he would go out and fight the Turks, if either the Emperor Frederick, or Charles of France, or Ladislas of Hungary or any other worthy prince would also join the war. Not one of those named has come forward.**
>
> **(*Commentaries*)**

THINGS TO DO

1 One theme which runs through the story of the Crusades is intolerance; whether the intolerance of the Crusaders to Islam or of the Eastern Christians to the Byzantines. Using newspapers and television reports, choose a story of conflict in the world today and write a report in which lessons learnt from the Crusades could help the situation.

2 Using an encyclopedia, write out the current year in Roman numerals, and to check if your answer is right, look at the end of one of the many television programmes where the year is also written this way. Now write the year using Arabic numerals. Which is easier to read? What else is much easier to do using Arabic rather than Roman numerals?

What kind of 'spiritual gifts' would the Pope offer? What evidence is there in this extract that there was little enthusiasm for Crusading by this time?

CAN YOU REMEMBER ?

Why England and France would not help Byzantium in the fifteenth century?
Why Frederick II was criticized by Muslims and Christians when he regained Jerusalem?
What happened to the Children's Crusade?

CHECK YOUR UNDERSTANDING

Can you remember the meaning of the following?

indulgence	concentric castles
heretic	inheritance
Papal blessing	

What can you remember?

Why did the First Crusade begin?
Why was Saladin admired?
Who were the 'Fighting Monks'?
What contribution did Anna Comnena make to our understanding of the Crusades?
How did the Franks hold on to their lands in Palestine after the First Crusade?
Why did the leaders of the Fourth Crusade attack Constantinople?
What did the Christian states of medieval Europe gain from the Crusades?
What was the nickname of Richard I of England?
Where is Constantinople on a modern map?

TIME CHART

AD 330 Constantine I divided the Roman Empire into two parts. The Eastern Roman Empire, with its capital at Constantinople, became known as Byzantium
1071 Battle of Manzikert
Seljuks capture Jerusalem
1095 Alexius I, Emperor of Byzantium, appeals to Europe for mercenaries. At Clermont, Pope Urban II preaches his Crusade
1096 The People's Crusade led by Peter the Hermit is destroyed
1096–99 The First Crusade
1099 Crusaders capture Jerusalem.
Kingdom of Jerusalem established.
1144 County of Edessa occupied by Muslims
1144–49 The Second Crusade fails
1187 Saladin destroys the army of Crusader occupation at the Battle of the Horns of Hattin
Jerusalem is captured by Saladin
Much of Crusader held land in Palestine overrun by Saladin
1189–92 The Third Crusade
1191 Richard I captures Acre
1192 Saladin and Richard I sign a five year truce.
Jerusalem remains in Muslim hands
1204 The Fourth Crusade. Crusaders and Venice take over Constantinople and divide between them the Byzantine Empire
Byzantines expelled to Nicaea
1212 The Children's Crusade
1217 St Louis of France leads Fifth Crusade
1221 Fifth Crusade fails
1229 Frederick II, Emperor of Germany regains Jerusalem by diplomacy
1248 The Crusade led by St Louis, King of France
1261 Byzantines return to Constantinople
AD 1291 Muslims capture Acre. Outremer ceases to exist
1453 Constantinople falls to the Ottoman Turks. The last emperor of Byzantium, Constantine XI, dies as the city is captured

Kings of The Kingdom of Jerusalem

1099 Godfrey of Lorraine
1100 Baldwin I
1118 Baldwin II
1131 Fulk and Queen Melisende
1143 Baldwin III
1162 Amalric
1174 Baldwin IV
1185 Baldwin V
1186 Guy of Lusignan and Queen Sibylla
1188 Guy (captured by Saladin at the Battle of Hattin)

The Muslim Near and Middle East in 1095.

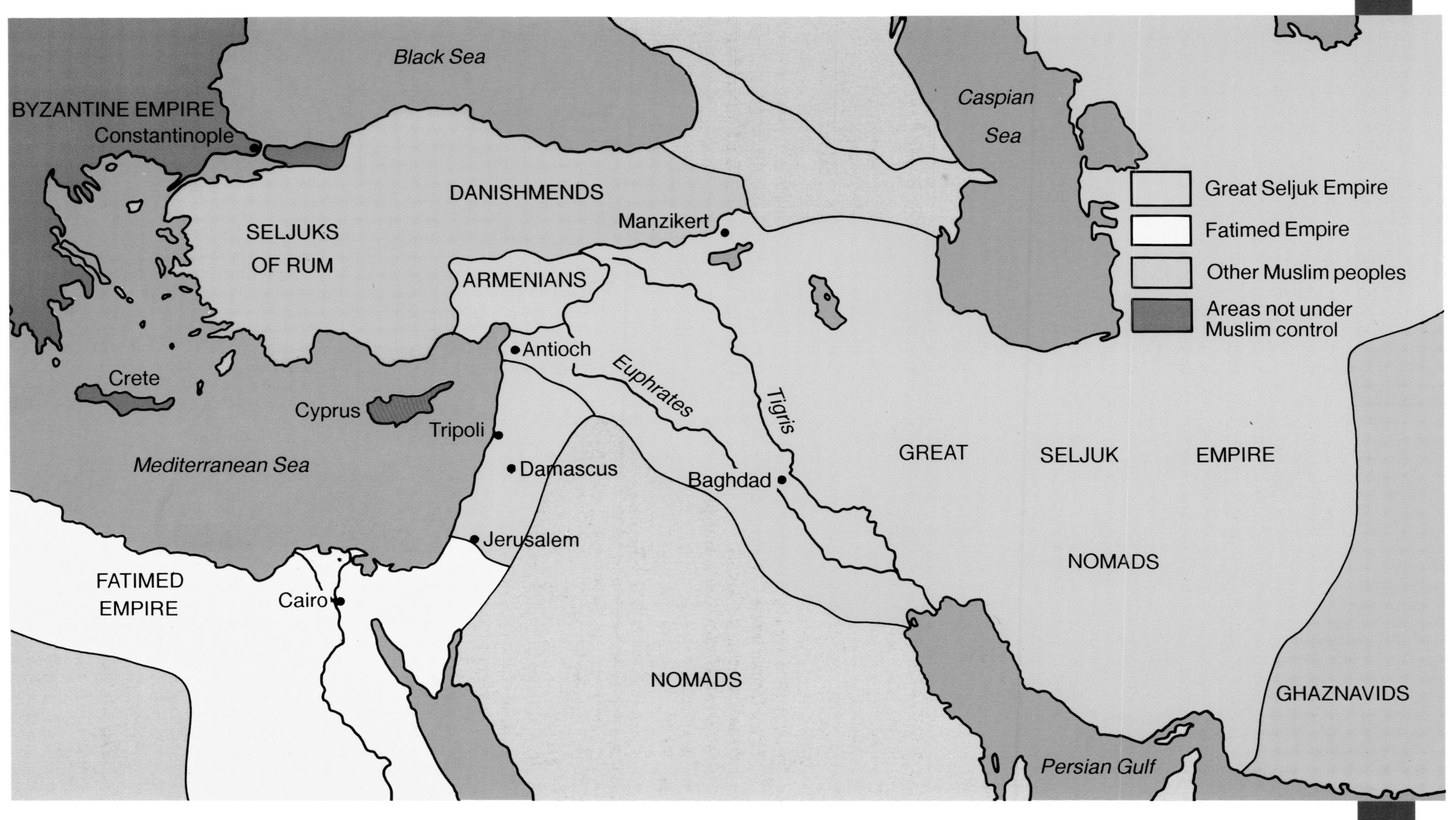

Black Sea
BYZANTINE EMPIRE
Constantinople
DANISHMENDS
SELJUKS
OF RUM
Manzikert
ARMENIANS
Caspian
Sea
Great Seljuk Empire
Fatimed Empire
Other Muslim peoples
Areas not under
Muslim control
Antioch
Euphrates
Tigris
Crete
Cyprus
Tripoli
Mediterranean Sea
Damascus
Baghdad
GREAT
SELJUK
EMPIRE
Jerusalem
FATIMED
EMPIRE
Cairo
NOMADS
NOMADS
GHAZNAVIDS
Persian Gulf

GLOSSARY

Assassins a Shiite sect from Persia (Iran) famous for their ability to kill important people
bigot one who is narrow-minded and intolerant
chivalry the medieval system by which knights, behaviour was conducted by a code of honour, courtesy and courage. Knights were expected to help defenceless people
Christendom Christian countries in Europe
consecration making a building, especially a church, sacred
Crusade an expedition to recover Jerusalem and the Holy Land from the Muslims, initiated and supported by the Christian Church
Crusader someone who goes on a Crusade
Eastern Orthodox Church the Byzantine 'state' religion; members were Christians but they did not share all the beliefs of the Roman Catholics or recognize the Pope as its head
elite a select band or group
entrepreneur an enterprising businessman
excommunication exclusion from membership of the Christian Church. This was a punishment handed out by Popes as a last resort which could affect individuals, communities or even states. After Venice captured Zara, Pope Innocent III excommunicated Venice and, for a while, the Crusaders. Medieval people dreaded this sanction as it meant, for example, they could not be buried properly with a service
exile someone who is forced to live outside their home country
Fatimids this Muslim branch was centred in Egypt, and regularly quarrelled with the Seljuks
fiefdom land given by a lord whose possessor owed allegiance to that lord
Franks crusaders who settled in Palestine
hashish a drug from the leaves of hemp, either smoked or chewed
heretic someone whose religious opinion is in conflict with the official beliefs of their religion
icon a painting regarded as sacred
Infidel a non-Christian
Latins another name for Crusaders
leprosy disease of the skin and nerves leading to deformities
mercenary a hired soldier
Patriarch a bishop
pilgrim someone who travels to a sacred place as an act of religious devotion
Pope head of the Christian Church
ransom money for buying the freedom of a prisoner
Roman Catholic Church the Christian religion of which the Pope is leader (father)
Seljuk Turks Sunni Muslims who defeated the Byzantines at Manzikert (1071) and occupied much of the Middle East as far south as Jerusalem
Shiites descendants of the supporters of Mohammed's cousin, Caliph (successor) Ali, who was murdered in 661 and succeeded by a member of the Umayyad family. Ali's supporters carried on fighting for his line until 680 when Ali's son, Hussein was killed. Today, the Shiites are a minority Islamic group and differ in some ways from the Sunni who follow the tradition of the Prophet
tolerance understanding and respect for beliefs and opinion of other people
truce temporary end of fighting
tribute money paid to an overlord or a conqueror, sometimes as 'protection'
usurper someone who seizes the crown wrongfully
vassal someone holding land on feudal principle of owing loyalty and duty to a superior

FURTHER READING

FOR YOUNGER PUPILS

Malcolm Billings, *The Cross and the Crescent*, BBC, 1987

J.A.P. Jones, *The Crusades*, Macmillan, 1984

John Jones, *The Medieval World*, Nelson, 1979

Peter Martin & Richard Pulley, *The Crusades*, Hodder and Stoughton, 1993

Ann Williams, *The Crusades* (Then & There series), Longman, 1988

FOR OLDER PUPILS

Elizabeth Hallam (editor), *Chronicles of the Crusades*, Weidenfeld, 1989

Joinville & Villehardouin, *Chronicles of the Crusades*, Penguin, 1963

Steven Runciman, *A History of the Crusades Vol I The First Crusade*, Cambridge University Press, 1951

Steven Runciman, *A History of the Crusades Vol II The Kingdom of Jerusalem*, Cambridge University Press, 1952

Steven Runciman, *A History of the Crusades Vol III The Kingdom of Acre*, Cambridge University Press, 1954

(Penguin have published a paperback edition)

Acknowledgements

The Author and Publishers would like to thank the following for their kind permission to reproduce illustrations: Aerofilms pages 29, 40; Ancient Art & Architecture Collection 38–9; Bibliothèque Nationale, Paris 28, 29; Bridgeman Art Library 16–17; British Library 6, 7, 8, 14, 16–17, 24–5, 25, 27 (both), 32–3, 40, 41; University of Edinburgh Library 4–5; Sonia Halliday frontispiece, 4, 9, 10, 12, 13, 16, 21, 22, 30, 33, 35; Scala 36; Swanston Graphics 34–5. The maps were drawn by Ken Smith.

INDEX